The Grown Woman's Guide

for Growing Spiritually in Christ

Over 20 Guided Prayers to Help You Through Grown Woman Issues

Kelley Hall

i

The Grown Woman's Guide for Growing Spiritually in Christ
ISBN: 978-1-7358344-1-2

Edited by Shawn Jackson
Photography by LaShay Price Photography
Cover by Design Place
Published by One2Mpower Publishing LLC

To the women in my family, my mother, daughter, sister, cousins, aunts, and all women around the world. May your spiritual life with Christ grow deeper than ever before.

TABLE OF CONTENTS

INTRODUCTION

Like so many women, I too, have recited lyrics to songs about being an independent woman. I love and bask in my womanhood. I enjoy the new developments I'm learning about myself, body, friendships, and relationships. There's a sense of freedom knowing I'm no longer a child and have the freedom to make my own decisions.

Yet no matter how many of your bills you can handle, or glasses of wine you can consume, no matter how many girlfriends you have in your corner, there is someone we must depend on. No matter if you're the type of woman that prefers six-inch heels, or would rather wear joggers every day, there is one who is the type for us all. His name is Jesus.

I've seen too many of my sisters in womanhood long for something more, search for answers about who they are, and desire to unbecome who they were all on their own. Self-help books may encourage you, however if you are a part of the problem, you need to seek help outside of yourself. Guidance from the Holy Spirit will lead you to true healing and wholeness, that you can't find within yourself. Sister, you no longer have to walk this journey alone! Your heavenly father wants to guide you through the issues, relationships, and celebrations that come with being a grown woman.

Once we have our spiritual life in order, we will notice a change in our hearts, and our homes. In order to grow spiritually, I believe there are four areas that we must become disciplined in: seeking God, taking in scripture, submitting, and serving. I've included these areas on each page to guide you! Here's a little more detailed description of what to expect.

Seeking God

One of the ways we can seek God is through prayer. In those moments, we can get still, silent, and hear what he has to say. Each page provides a bit of discussion and a prayer prompt to cover you and help you start your prayers when you don't know what to say. I wrote them as the Holy Spirit gave them to me. It is my hope that they help you press into his presence more, for yourself, those in your circle, and other women around the world.

Taking in Scripture

Reading God's word and letting it abide in our hearts can expand our knowledge of who he is. I've provided scriptures for various scenarios we may face and pray that you hold them in your heart. Rewrite them, study them, and recite them for yourself.

Submitting

This one can get tough and takes prayer, but I believe we can grow spiritually mature when we truly submit. Each page will provide a space in which you can write down how you plan to submit to God in a certain area of your life. Write out any takeaway from the discussion I share or scriptures you read. I also include a question or two in the discussion section to help you process what you should submit to God.

Serving

I believe serving is vital to our spiritual walk. It helps us take the focus off ourselves and look to the needs of others. Each page contains suggestions on how or where to serve.

WARRIOR WITHIN YOU

As a worshipper/musician and warrior, I truly believe in the power of prayer! I've seen what it can do. Instead of making this a 20, 30, or 100-day devotional, God laid it on my heart to include various issues and scenarios we face so that the days of the week won't matter. While this isn't a book that guarantees everything will go your way, it is a release of faith into the atmosphere and an agreement with God. Ladies we don't need the crystals or astrology signs to direct us. We have a God who's omnipresent, and desires to be involved in every detail of our life. One thing I will forever stand by no matter how hard it is to submit to, is praying "Not my will Lord, but your will be done." When we pray, "Your will be done," we are submitting to whatever outcome he provides. My hope is that you will get to the place of seeking him fully, reading scriptures, submitting your issues to him, and serving others. May you be blessed and share this book with your loved ones..

SEEKING GOD FOR SALVATION

I believe we are as close to God as we want to be. What's your prayer life like? Do you have one? Do you have a favorite scripture? Although I can't see your response, take a moment to write it down. This will allow you to really see where you are spiritually and what areas you could grow in.

If you answered no and don't have a relationship with Jesus, then I want to invite you to one of the most important **prayer prompts**!

This is one that leads you to the gift of salvation. Salvation and growing spiritually is not just attending church every Sunday or attending Bible study. Growing spiritually starts with your relationship of knowing Jesus. A lot of us are good at speaking "Christianese." We say the churchy things we've heard our grandparents or guardians say, but we leave out the relationship and the faith that is required. Personally, having a relationship with Jesus means I can talk to him like I would my biological father. I don't have to say words like "thou, thee," or anything that sounds like I'm from the B.C. era. I can literally sit on my bed and discuss my day with him, and he will listen and respond.

I encourage you to let him in and be (respectfully) blunt with him. Here are a few things I want you to realize:

- He wants to hear from you.

- You are good enough to have a relationship with him; there is nothing too dirty that will keep you from him.
- He not only gives you time for growth, but he also helps you grow.
- There is a warrior within you.

Prayer Prompt

God, I ask that you come into my heart so that I can truly discover who you are and the woman I am becoming. I want to know you more and experience your love. Lord, help me walk into the fullness of who I am as you prune the things that don't belong. I confess that you are Lord. I believe in the Father, Son, and Holy Spirit. I surrender fully to you now and believe that I will learn how to trust you completely. I'm ready to become the mature woman you've called me to be. I want to grow spiritually and ask that you forgive me of my sins and make me brand new. In Jesus' name. Amen.

If you prayed that prayer, then please know I and all of heaven are rejoicing! Read these scriptures below to see what the Bible says about salvation. Remember, you are still free, actually freer. You're still independent and now stronger because you've made the best choice!

Scriptures on Salvation

Luke 15:7 (NIV) "I say to you that likewise there will be more joy in heaven over one sinner who repents than over ninety-nine just persons who need no repentance."

John 3:16 (KJV) "For God so loved the world, that he gave his only begotten Son, that whosoever believeth in him, should not perish but have everlasting life."

Romans 10:9 (NIV) "If you declare with your mouth, Jesus is Lord, and believe in your heart that God raised him from the dead, you will be saved."

Romans 10:11 (NIV) "Anyone who believes in me will never be put to shame."

Submit

Write down three areas you'd like to see yourself grow in spiritually. It could be reading scriptures, prayer, learning more history about the bible. What do you feel is hindering you?

_____

_____

_____

_____

Serve

Find someone to share your faith with. Lead them into a prayer of salvation.

Welcome to your new beginning!

SEEKING GOD FOR DISCERNMENT

I often hear women discuss our knowledge of having intuition. We just know or have a gut feeling about a person or situation that doesn't seem right. We are quick to say when something is just off; yet even with our intuition, we may find ourselves feeling confused. We wonder if we were right or wrong. This is why grown women need spiritual discernment too. Not just this said "gut superpower" we feel we possess.

Let's be honest; we still make the wrong choices if there isn't guidance from the Holy Spirit that we need. There is spiritual warfare going on all around us, and we need to seek God on how to deal with it. His guidance will not confuse us or steer us in the wrong direction. His guidance is trustworthy and clear and goes beyond the old wives' tales of our ancestors and beyond what an epiphany can tell us. The Father can open our spiritual eyes to seeing attacks before they come.

Prayer Prompt

Lord, thank you for creating us with intuition. We ask that you take this ability and strengthen it and develop it into discernment. Help us to take heed to what your spirit says about a person, place, or anything we question in our lives. Reveal to us what your will is and help us to navigate between the spiritual and the natural. We will look to you for answers, and not deep within ourselves because you are all knowing, and all seeing. Thank you, for opening our hearts to hear from you. In Jesus name. Amen.

Scriptures on Discernment

Psalm 25:4-5 (NIV) "Show me your ways, Lord, teach me your paths. Guide me in your truth and teach me, for you are God my Savior, and my hope is in you all day long."

1 John 4:1 (ESV) "Beloved, do not believe every spirit, but test the spirits to see whether they are from God, for many false prophets have gone out into the world."

Philippians 1:9 (NKJV) "And it is my prayer that your love may abound more and more, with knowledge and all discernment, so that you may approve what is excellent, and so be pure and blameless for the day of Christ."

Hebrews 5:14 (ESV) "But solid food is for the mature, for those who have their powers of discernment trained by constant practice to distinguish good from evil."

Submit

Write down the two areas that you're seeking clarity in. It could be a relationship, career change, or moving to a new location.

_____

_____

_____

_____

Serve

Ask someone how you can pray for God's direction in their life.

SEEKING GOD WHEN OVERWHELMED

For some of us, the heavy workflow is becoming too much, added with maybe wearing too many hats as a wife, single parent, boss, or employee. Some of us are overwhelmed as singles with full-fledged careers, and then there are those of us who are praying for direction and feel useless. No matter which title or bracket you fit in, being overwhelmed comes for us all.

The problem is we try to handle everything on our own. We boost ourselves up, and say we can handle it all, instead of asking God how things should be handled. Just because something is your responsibility or part of your normal routine, doesn't mean you should leave God out of it.

Personally, as a single mother of two, going to school and starting my music career has left me drained at times. When I'm depleted and can't go on, I find that the Father's arms are the most comforting. Yes, self-care, hobbies, and time alone are good, however if I don't take my load to God in prayer, I will eventually become depleted. Warrior you don't have to carry it all.

Prayer Prompt

Father, I'm so overwhelmed. You know how much I have on my plate, and I admit some of these things I've added thinking they would help me seem busier or important. God, right now, I need you to ease these overwhelming thoughts, the stress, and the tension in my life. Please show me a way out. Show me how to plan and schedule things better and bring the right mentors in my life. Show me how to be productive and find rest, so that I'm not angry, sad, or weak. Thank you for helping me find moments of self-care and solitude. In Jesus' name. Amen.

Scriptures on Being Overwhelmed

Isaiah 40:31 (NKJV) "But those who wait on the Lord shall renew their strength; they shall mount up on wings as eagles; they shall run and not grow weary; they shall walk, and not faint."

Matthew 11:28 (NIV) "Come to me, all you who are weary and burdened, and I will give you rest."

Hebrews 12:2-3 (NIV)"...fixing our eyes on Jesus the pioneer and perfecter of faith. For the joy set before him he endured the cross, scorning its shame, and sat down at the right hand of the throne of God. Consider him who endured such opposition from sinners, so that you will not grow weary and lose heart."

Submit

Write down four things you can omit or rearrange that will leave you less overwhelmed?

_____

_____

_____

_____

Serve

Find a new mother to offer a meal, prayer, or a hand so that she's less overwhelmed.

SEEKING GOD FOR JOY

Most children find joy easy to come by. Even when faced with obstacles, they are more optimistic and willing to look on the bright side. Life comes at us fast, and we may find it hard to receive joy, especially the joy of the Lord. I've known women who have tried to obtain joy by being in a relationship (it's me; I was that woman). I have friends that thought they could obtain joy through jobs, clothes, and houses; however, those things just can't satisfy. While there is nothing wrong with having nice things, your dream job, entrepreneurship, and relationships, we must first allow Jesus to be the foundation of our joy. When he is our joy the temporary things don't matter as much. We won't be easily moved or sink down into depression when we have God as the center of our joy. This doesn't mean we won't feel sad due to loss, grief, or a bad day, however we will know who fills us back up. Our satisfaction won't be in material things, or people that change like the wind.

Prayer Prompt

Father God, I ask today that you restore the joy in my sister's heart. I cast down everything that has tried to make her feel dark and cold. I come against every high thing and imagination that is restricting her from the fullness of the joy you give. Lord, we thank you that you are the ultimate void filler and joy filler; everything else is added. We thank you that we will begin to smile, dance, and truly enjoy life to the fullest. Help us to forgive, let go of bitterness, and anything that is not of you. In Jesus' name. Amen.

Scriptures on Joy

Psalm 32:11 (NIV) "Rejoice in the Lord and be glad, you righteous; sing, all you who are upright in heart."

Psalm 30:5 (KJV) "For his anger endureth but for a moment; in his favor is life: weeping may endure for a night, but joy cometh in the morning."

John 15:10-11 (NIV) "If you keep my commands, you will remain in my love, just as I have kept my Father's commands and remain in his love. I have told you this so that my joy may be in you and that your joy may be complete."

Submit

Write down three things that aren't materialistic that bring you joy. Ask God to bring increase in these areas.

_____

_____

_____

_____

Serve

Bring someone joy by leaving them a sweet Post-it note, text message, or email.

SEEKING GOD WHEN GUILT TRIPPING

I remember a time I entered into a season of life where almost everything from my past decided to come for me. I thought about those I've disappointed, hurt, or let down even if unintentionally. I would overthink about the times I back slide and wonder how God could forgive me. The scenarios ran through my mind at times so much I could barely sleep. I began to seek God, and he led me to change my mindset, forgive myself, and receive the forgiveness he so freely gives.

If you're in a season of your life where you keep replaying your past and thinking about various things you should, could, would have done differently whether marriage, divorce, regretting the abortion, mom guilt, financial decisions, etc., I want to challenge you today to lay it ALL down! God wants all the heaviness. As a matter of fact, he already paid for it, and salvation is your way out! There is no condemnation in Christ. His desire is not for you to replay everything you've done wrong. His desire for you is forgiveness, and freedom. Pray with the Prayer Prompt, and let's change this mindset.

Prayer Prompt

Lord, please deliver me from replaying the past. Please reset my mind and way of thinking. Help me to let go of the worldly mindset that keeps me bound. Help me to focus on the right things as your word says, that are pure, lovely, and noble. I thank you, Father, that the enemy has no say in my life, and every twisted truth is bound. I thank you for helping me to meditate on things above and celebrate my growth in you. I receive your forgiveness and know that your death was not in vain. In Jesus' name. Amen.

Scriptures That Relieve Guilt

Ephesians 1:7 (NIV) "In him we have redemption through his blood, the forgiveness of sins, in accordance with the riches of God's grace."

Hebrews 10:22-23 (NIV) "Let us draw near to God with a sincere heart and with the full assurance that faith brings, having our hearts sprinkled to cleanse us from a guilty conscience and having our bodies washed with pure water. Let us hold unswervingly to the hope we profess, for he who promised is faithful."

Psalm 103:12 (KJV) "As far as the east is from the west, so far hath he removed our transgressions from us."

Submit

Repeat these affirmations to denounce guilt. Rewrite them as a declaration.

- God has paid the price for my sins.
- I've taken ownership of my sins, and I am forgiven.
- I am not defined by my past.
- Whom the Son sets free is free indeed.

Serve

Pray that those within the prison system will open their hearts to God's love and salvation.

SEEKING GOD TO BE SET APART

What do you believe it means to be grown and set apart? You're now at the age where you're grown enough to do whatever you desire, does this mean you do it? God is not requiring perfection, he doesn't expect you to be like the minister you see on television, or to obtain a theology degree. Those positions aren't for everybody; however, he does require a willing heart. This means saying no to things you once easily said yes to. It will require a mind set on being righteous, a mouth that is gossip free, a mindset that doesn't think like the world. Being set apart will also require boldness to push past opinions of those who say, "you're acting different". The more you press into his presence, the more you will notice your desires change. It doesn't matter if you're known to be the one who "turns up" or if you're usually the first one to cuss someone out. You may be well-known for your certain ways for years, but I encourage you, to lean into the tug that says it's time for a change. Are you willing to be set apart? He is able to help you.

Prayer Prompt

Lord, help your daughters to understand what it means to be set apart. Help us to say no to things that we shouldn't be a part of, even if we're grown enough to do them. Help us in those moments of weakness and keep us on the path to righteousness. We trust you and will walk on the narrow path, even if there's only a few others on it. Thank you, Lord, for delivering us from our old ways, and that you deliver us from desiring to fit in. In Jesus' name. Amen.

Scriptures for Staying Set Apart

Psalm 25:4-5 (NIV) "Show me your ways, Lord teach me your paths. Guide me in your truth and teach me, for you are my God my Savior, and my hope is in you all day long."

Matthew 7:13 (NKJV) "Enter by the narrow gate; for wide is the gate and broad that leads to destruction, and there are many who enter through it."

Romans 12:2 (NIV) "Do not conform to the pattern of this world but be transformed by the renewing of your mind. Then you will be able to test and approve what God's will is his good, pleasing and perfect will."

Submit

Write a list of things you enjoy doing that makes you feel most alive, yet don't require compromising your faith.

_____

_____

_____

_____

Serve

Set an example to others showing how you are set apart, yet still enjoy life. Share virtually or with a group of close friends.

SEEKING GOD FOR PURITY

I recently created videos for my YouTube channel titled "The Soul Tie Series." In these videos, I shared my testimony about overcoming a soul tie. I also shared what insecurities lead me to the bed that caused the soul tie. As a grown woman, we will deal with feelings that come naturally. It's not a sin to desire sex and intimacy. It is normal to want to give and receive affection, no deliverance required. So why purity? Although God has given us free will, when we give him our yes, we give that free will back to him and surrender. Purity isn't just a movement or a commitment for singles. There's a mindset married couples should have, to keep their eyes from wandering and minds from being impure. Purity was honestly hard for me at first because I knew that meant the possibility of being single and abstaining forever. I knew I was no longer in control of my own love life. Yet, I trusted that God knows the desires of my heart. He knows you so well; he won't let you down. Strongholds may come from something that happened to you or from looking at pornography or having sinful nature. God can heal you from the lust, soul tie, and stronghold. This is a battle you won't face alone. You can be made whole.

Prayer Prompt

Lord, help my sisters in Christ to calm every burning desire. Help us break bad habits and know our worth. We thank you that our mindsets will change, and we won't give in to every temptation. Break the soul ties that we've allowed to form, break the cycles that have become our normal. Send us righteous accountability partners or place us in a bible study group that will help us grow. Allow us to see our worth and see ourselves the way you see us. Help us fix our eyes on the right things, correct our thoughts, and allow us to trade all filthy rags, for purity. In Jesus' name. Amen.

Scriptures on Purity

1 Corinthians 6:18-20 (NIV) "Flee from sexual immorality. All other sins a person commits are outside the body, but whoever sins sexually, sins against their own body. Do you not know that your bodies are temples of the Holy Spirit, who is in you, whom you have received from God? You are not your own; you were bought at a price. Therefore, honor God with your bodies."

Thessalonians 4:3-5 (NIV) "It is God's will that you should be sanctified: that you should avoid sexual immorality, that each of you should learn to control your own body in a way that is holy and honorable, not in passionate lust like pagans, who do not know God."

1 Corinthians 10:13 (NIV) "No temptation has overtaken you except what is common to mankind. And God is faithful; he

will not let you be tempted beyond what you can bear. But when you are tempted, he will also provide a way out so that you can endure it."

Submit

What are some things that you can delete out of your life that will help you flee from sexual strongholds? Write down what this looks like for you.

_____

_____

_____

_____

Serve

Find a friend that will hold you accountable and one you can help hold accountable as you seek a life of purity.

SEEKING GOD FOR HEALING

Whether it's the common cold or diagnosis we didn't see coming, sickness is something we should hand over to Jesus. Instead of Googling symptoms, burning sage, and seeking worldly ways of healing, we can stand on what his word says. I want to encourage you to lay hands on yourself and any areas you're experiencing pain or illness. The word of God says, "by his stripes we are healed." Your testimony begins when you believe, claim, rebuke, and speak those things that aren't as if they were. It doesn't matter if it's allergies or results from a CAT scan or MRI; there is nothing too hard for God. I'm a witness to the outcome of praying and interceding for myself. When believing God for a miracle, you must show up in faith. That may mean not speaking negative over your life, and not sharing all the negative details with people. Instead go into your prayer closet and repeat healing scriptures, rejoice in the midst of the pain, and see yourself healed. We may not always receive the outcome that we desire, but because we know he is God, he will have the best outcome for us. Find other believers who will stand in the gap for you, and claim healing for yourself, family, and friends.

Prayer Prompt

Father, your word says life and death are in the power of the tongue. I pray that my sisters in Christ will use their bold minds and tongues to proclaim healing over themselves and their loved ones. I pray they won't just stay down and stagnant even when they feel weak. Please help them to proclaim healing scriptures and repeat them until they see the miracles manifest. I pray they will know you are powerful, and they will please you with their faith. In Jesus' name. Amen.

Scriptures on Healing

Isaiah 53:4-5 (NIV) "Surely he took up our pain and bore our suffering, yet we considered him punished by God, stricken by him, and afflicted. But he was pierced for our transgressions, he was crushed for our iniquities; the punishment that brought us peace was on him, and by his wounds we are healed."

Jeremiah 30:17 (NIV) "But I will restore you to health and heal your wounds, declares the Lord, because you are called an outcast, Zion for whom no one cares."

James 5:14-15 (NIV) "Is anyone among you sick? Let them call the elders of the church to pray over them and anoint them with oil in the name of the Lord. And the prayer offered in faith will make the sick person well; the Lord will raise them up. If they have sinned, they will be forgiven."

1 Peter 2:24 (NIV) "He himself bore our sins" in his body on the cross, so that we might die to sins and live for righteousness; by his wounds you are healed."

Submit

Write down your favorite scriptures that pertain to healing. Meditate on them as they manifest

_____

_____

_____

_____

Serve

Find someone to come into agreement with for their healing. Share your favorite healing scripture with them.

SEEKING GOD FOR PATIENCE IN WAITING

I can remember turning twenty-five and panicking about not yet reaching my goal of marriage by that age. I can giggle about it now, however, at the time it was a serious concern. I have friends who are concerned about not yet having kids and wondering when or if it will happen. I know women who are yearning for that next step in their career to come, but they're told they don't have enough experience yet, and then there's those who wish time would slow down because they feel they are running out of time. I want to encourage you that you are right where you need to be. Even if you took a wrong turn, God was already aware. He was there in the past, here in the present, and will be with you in the future. Having a timeline looks good on paper, and wanting to become a wife, mother, boss, may be something that the Father also wants for you. During the waiting season, you can ask God to align your will with his. Ask him what he wants you to learn as you wait. See what he's taking away, and how he's preparing you, even though it may be hard.

Prayer Prompt

Heavenly Father, remind us that you are Lord over time and space. There are no limits to what you can do, doors you can open or close. Help us to stop panicking or obsessing over what's next and to trust that whatever season we are currently in is ripe for learning, growing, and harvest. Calm our nerves that tell us time is running out or that we're too young. We thank you ultimately for peace, patience, and longsuffering. In Jesus' name. Amen.

Scriptures on Waiting

Isaiah 40:31 (KJV) "But they that wait upon the Lord shall renew their strength; they shall mount up with wings as eagles; they shall run, and not be weary; they shall walk, and not faint."

Psalm 90:4 (NIV) "A thousand years in your sight are like a day that has just gone by, or like a watch in the night."

Psalm 27:13-14 (NIV) "I remain confident of this: I will see the goodness of the Lord in the land of the living. Wait for the Lord; be strong and take heart and wait for the Lord."

Submit

Write out four goals you will focus on and submit to God. Keep track of your growth.

_____

_____

_____

_____

Serve

Help a church or a friend with reaching a goal via donations or time.

SEEKING GOD FOR BOLDNESS

Have you ever had to present a presentation at school or work and could literally feel yourself shaking? Maybe your body even responds with a bit of sweat and overthinking. I remember hearing a friend of mine share about her journey of becoming a Toastmaster speaker. For those of you not familiar, Toastmasters is an event where you connect with other speakers in your community and basically present various speaking topics, and work on your speech and presentation. My friend started off nervous, shaking, and maybe even a little sweaty, yet she persisted. She continued to show up, speak and present, competing against others, and eventually went on to win not only in her community but at a regional event! As a woman of faith, she prayed and persisted! Ladies, I want to encourage you that if boldness is an area of struggle for you, God can give you the courage and strength you need to persevere. He literally cares about every detail that concerns you. He cares about your nerves at the job interview, the adoption process, giving birth, or breaking out of your comfort zone to do all that he's called you to do! Every movement may not feel like a moment to roar in, but I want to challenge you to seek God for strength and wisdom and see the bold woman in the mirror.

Prayer Prompt

God, thank you that your daughters were born with a built-in roar! Even those of us who feel shy compared to most can show up as warriors when needed. Help us to tap into that boldness that only you can give that will strengthen us to speak up and use our voices as you desire us to. Help us break away from being timid, overlooked, or weak. Give us the wisdom to know when to speak and the boldness that it takes to be silent in some situations where an argument may arise. Thank you for boldness on the job interview, the presentation, or whatever may require us to be fierce. Lord, give us the boldness to witness to others, serve and love. Give us the boldness to lay down what is not of you and to speak up and be who you've called us to be. In Jesus' name. Amen.

Scriptures on Boldness

Hebrews 12:1-2 (NIV) "Therefore since we are surrounded by such a great cloud of witness, let us throw off everything that hinders and the sin that so easily entangles. And let us run with perseverance the race marked out for us, fixing our eyes on Jesus, the pioneer and perfecter of faith. For the joy set before him he endured on the cross, scorning its shame, and sat down at the right hand of the throne of God."

Philippians 4:13 (NIV) "I can do all this through him who gives me strength."

1 Corinthians 16:13 (NIV) "Be on guard; stand firm in the faith; be courageous and strong."

Submit

Write down 3 areas that you desire God to help you be bold in. Submit these areas to him.

_____

_____

_____

_____

Serve

Boldly serve a ministry, business, or your boss by trying something out of your comfort zone. Ask for a task outside of your normal.

SEEKING GOD'S HELP WITH PERFECTION

The desire to look as if we have it all together is one that comes easily, especially in the type of world we're in now. Society tells us that we will have more success, fame, friends if we do x, y, and z, and that having fame, lots of friends, and success means we've reached a certain type of status in life. We strive for perfection to be seen and to have status on social media, yet could help so many others, if we share our truth. We believe that if we don't have enough likes, followers, and responses, we are not enough. This can cause us to compare ourselves to friends and even people we should look up to. We must understand that there is beauty in brokenness, courage in being content, and a testimony that can be shared just by staying true to ourselves. We must ask that he remove the blinders that tell us we aren't enough as we are.

Prayer Prompt

Father God, we ask in the mighty name of Jesus that you remove the blinders and block the mindset that tells us we aren't enough. Help us to stop striving for status or to be seen. Take the desire for perfection and teach us what it means to be holy and righteous, even in our brokenness. Help us to take off the mask, causing us to strive, prove, or desire attention. Help us to rest in knowing that we are enough as we are and any growth, we need must come from you. In Jesus' name. Amen.

Scriptures When Struggling with Perfection

2 Corinthians 12:8-10 (KJV) "My grace is sufficient for you, for my strength is made perfect in weakness."

Psalm 139:14 (NIV) "I praise you because I am fearfully and wonderfully made; your works are wonderful; I know that full well."

Submit

Where does your desire for perfection come from? Write a journal entry asking God to help you with the desire for perfection.

_____

_____

_____

_____

Serve

Find a local food pantry or shelter in need of assistance to serve at.

SEEKING GOD FOR A STRONGER PRAYER LIFE

Finding time to spend with Jesus is sometimes easier said than done. We live busy lives with children, spouses, work, entrepreneurship, or as singles with social lives and careers. Disciplining ourselves to spend thirty minutes with Jesus can seem hard, but I encourage you to find a starting point. Try praying for ten minutes on Monday, twenty minutes on Tuesday, and increase that time each day. I can recall starting my prayer life out with just a few moments, and sometimes that included saying my grace over food. Then I begin to see mentors that I admired speak about spending hours in prayer or waking up before sunrise to pray. I also can recall my own mother, who spent hours in prayer, reading scripture, and anointing the house throughout my childhood and even now. I praise God I've been able to see the fruit and manifestation of those prayers. When I was younger, I couldn't picture having a prayer life of my own like my mother or mentors; however, I realized the more I carved out time to spend with him, the more I longed for him. I began to get disciplined, and before I knew it, I too was spending thirty minutes or longer in his presence. God is not looking at a watch when you come to him. All he desires is time with you, even if it is a focused five minutes. I challenge you to go deeper into his presence so you will see a harvest in your heart. This is a sacred time you can place your desires, deepest concerns, and all that you are at his feet.

Prayer Prompt

Lord God, help us to seek you more! I pray that my sisters in Christ will see you as priority and will sit in your presence more each day. I pray they will say yes when you wake them earlier than they are used to and that your voice will speak to them as they read your word. I pray they will study and allow your words to abide in their hearts. Help us to stop scrolling through the distractions of social media, and to build a prayer life that will produce faith, healing, and a deeper relationship with you. In Jesus' name. Amen.

Scriptures for a Stronger Prayer Life

2 Timothy 2:15 (AMP) "Study and do your best to present yourself to God approved, a workman [tested by trial] who has no reason to be ashamed, accurately handling and skillfully teaching the word of truth."

John 15:4 (ESV) "Abide in me, and I in you. As the branch cannot bear fruit by itself, unless it abides in the vine, neither can you, unless you abide in me."

James 4:8 (NIV) "Come near to God and he will come near to you. Wash your hands, you sinners, and purify you hearts, you double-minded."

Submit

Write down two ways you plan to increase your prayer life.

_____

_____

_____

_____

Serve

Offer to pray on a prayer line, group, or for someone God places on your heart.

SEEKING GOD FOR HEALING FROM THE PAST

Healing from your past is so vital to becoming all God created you to be. The journey won't be easy, but it will be worth it. If your heart is open to healing and forgiveness, then he will guide you to freedom. For some, he may use therapy, and there is nothing to be ashamed of. There are Christian therapists that can provide medical and spiritual help for your healing. The Holy Spirit may intercede, healing you supernaturally, and that process may involve forgiving yourself and just crying out to him. Healing will require you to get out of your comfort zone and will stretch you in many ways. You will experience various emotions, but the wounds will begin to close as he makes you whole. Make up your mind, that this month won't be like the last, start searching for the right therapist. Reach out to a counselor at church, pray to become more aware of your triggers, and how to avoid them. Allow God to redeem and restore you.

Prayer Prompt

Father God, in John 4, we read about how you met the Samaritan woman at the well; you told her that you knew all about her past and how she was living. You gave her an invitation that would change her life. I pray that the women who are reading this will receive this invitation to draw closer to you for their healing and restoration. Please show them how you give beauty for ashes, may they seek you for healing from brokenness, bitterness, and trauma. Break off every chain holding them back and show them a glimpse of freedom until it is complete. In Jesus' name. Amen.

Scriptures on Healing from your Past

Psalm 37:5-6 (NIV) "Commit your way unto the Lord; trust in him and he will do this: He will make your righteous reward shine like the dawn, your vindication like the noonday."

Micah 7:18 (NIV) "Who is God like you, who pardons sin and forgives the transgression of the remnant of his inheritance? You do not stay angry forever but delight to show mercy."

John 4:13-14 (NIV) "Jesus answered, everyone who drinks this water will be thirsty again, but whoever drinks the water I give them will never thirst. Indeed, the water I give them will become in them a spring of water welling up to eternal life."

Submit

What steps will you take to receive healing from your past? Is therapy something you're interested in? Write down 4 things you will do to move forward from your past.

_____

_____

_____

_____

Serve

Learn the love language of a family member or friend. Serve them through it.

SEEKING GOD FOR MINDFULNESS

The thoughts that we think can cause hindrances or help propel us into greatness. The words that we speak over our lives are powerful, and it's so imperative that we are mindful of what comes out of our mouths, but it starts in our mind. This is why even as grown women we should be so careful about what we view and what we listen to.

Not long ago, I had a conversation with a sister who shared with me that she had to stop listening to a certain artist because she was starting to see the negative effects of the music in her life. She could tell that the music and even movements from this artist were becoming too worldly and demonic. I shared with her that my sentiments were the same, and I, too, no longer listened to this artist when God began to change my life. While it may not be a sin to listen to secular artists, we must be careful about what we allow in our eye and ear gates. They can open doors to how we think, what we desire, and how we react. It usually seeps in without us really noticing. Thankfully, as you draw closer to God, he will open your mind to more of this, then it's up to you to make the change.

Prayer Prompt

Help us, Holy Spirit, to get free from our normal routine of listening and watching whatever is popular or just anything that interests us. Help us to be the mature women after your heart, imperfect yet set apart. Help us to be mindful of what we are actually doing and not to jump on every trend that is set before us. Deliver us from distractions and help us to focus on developing a Christ like mindset. Remove the toxins from things we allowed and purify our souls. We ask these things in the name of Jesus. Amen.

Scripture for Mindfulness

Philippians (4:8 NIV) "Finally brothers and sisters, whatever is true, whatever is noble, whatever is right, whatever is pure, whatever is lovely, whatever is admirable if anything is excellent or praiseworthy think about such things.

Proverbs 4:23-27 (NIV) Above all else guard your heart, for everything you do flows from it. Keep your mouth free of perversity; keep corrupt talk far from your lips. Let your eyes look straight ahead; fix your gaze directly before you. Give careful thought to the paths for your feet and be steadfast in all your ways. Do not turn to the right or the left; keep your foot from evil.

Submit

Write down three ways you can be more mindful of what you entertain.

_____

_____

_____

_____

Serve

Send an encouraging song to a friend or relative.

SEEKING GOD FOR VICTORY AND PEACE

A rough week at home or work may leave you feeling defeated. You may find yourself questioning your life, and purpose. If you're not careful, you'll sink further into depression, while the enemy has a field day with your mind. The only way to stop this is by acknowledging that you are not alone, and God is present, even though it doesn't feel like it. You must also learn how to have a victorious mindset. Your bad day is not the end of the world, that disappointment will not last and this too shall pass. Every thought that enters your mind must be accounted for, producing peace, and solutions. If you're on the job, whisper to yourself, "I have the victory." If you're at home yell "Victory is mine." If you're at school, write it down over several times. Victory is already yours, and Christ has already overcome.

Prayer Prompt

Lord, we thank you for victory! Though we may face battles, we will not be defeated, and even when the circumstances try to tell us differently, you will remind your daughters of the victorious mindset we have in you. Show us we can still have joy, peace, and strength no matter what. Let us declare victory over our day, over our family, our health, and finances in your mighty name. Amen.

Scriptures on Victory

John 16:33 (NIV) "I have told you these things, so that in me you may have peace. In this world you will have trouble. But take heart! I have overcome the world."

Romans 8:31-32 (NIV) "What, then shall we say in response to these things? If God is for us, who can be against us?"

1 Corinthians 15:57 (ESV) "But thanks be to God, who gives us the victory through our Lord Jesus Christ."

Submit

Write down a moment that started with feelings of defeat, that God turned into victory. This will help you remember his faithfulness.

_____

_____

_____

_____

Serve

Ask a friend or relative how you can help declare victory for them.

SEEKING GOD WHEN TEMPTED

Wondering if you should text that ex that you know God pulled you away from? Struggling with whether or not to do the right thing at work? Have you found yourself tempted to buy things in order to keep up with social media trends? Maybe none of these are an area of struggle, maybe you've been tempted with overindulging in food or mishandling finances.

Trust me, we've all been tempted, and this is something that even Jesus had to deal with (Matthew 4:1-11). Being tempted is not a sin; we live in fleshly human bodies and were born into a sinful world. What we need to be mindful of is our reaction and response to temptation. Just because an opportunity presents itself doesn't mean we should take it. There are times when saying no will be the best answer, even if it doesn't please someone. Father God will help us in our areas of weakness, even when we mess up.

Prayer Prompt

Father, help us when we are tempted. Help us to keep our mind on you and our purpose. Guide us on when to say yes, and when to say no. Provide us the wisdom we need to rebuke things that aren't good for us. Give us grace when we do give in to temptation. Amen.

Scriptures that help to deal with temptation

Matthew 26:41 (NIV) "Watch and pray so that you will not fall into temptation. The spirit is willing, but the flesh is weak."

1 Corinthians 10:13 (NIV) "No temptation has overtaken you except what is common to mankind. And God is faithful; he will not let you be tempted beyond what you can bear. But when you are tempted, he will also provide a way out so that you can endure it."

2 Corinthians 12:9 (NIV) "My Grace is sufficient for you, for my power is made perfect in weakness."

2 Corinthians 12:10 (NIV) "That is why, for Christ's sake, I delight in weaknesses, in insults, in hardships, in persecutions, in difficulties. For when I am weak, then I am strong."

Submit

Be honest with yourself about the things you're tempted by. Write at least three areas of struggle and ask God to show you a way out.

_____

_____

_____

_____

Serve

Pray for those dealing with addictions that God will help them recover fully and resist temptation.

SEEKING GOD FOR REFUGE

Imagine having a daddy that covers you and makes you so secure that every doubt has to run and flee. Imagine being able to trust and just know that you're taken care of and that you are highly protected by a mighty Savior and his army of angels. I want you to know that this is your reality. God is our hiding place, our security, our mighty fortress, protector, and keeper. We may have enemies in this life on earth and in the spiritual realm, but the weapons from them will not ever prosper. Have faith, believing that you are covered. Look back over your life at how he has kept you thus far. He has never failed you. I know circumstances can bring about fear and uncertainty, and at times we may not see our way out of hard circumstances. The truth is though, he is already covering us, even though we can't see him. He is working all things out and will turn it around for his glory. We have no reason to worry about what's next, how things will work out, or about being harmed. Our God is a present help.

Prayer Prompt

Lord, we come to you seeking refuge. Some of us didn't grow up with a father, and even if we had a stepfather or good men in our lives, no one compares to you. Your covering is forever, and your love never fails us. Help us to stop living in fear and take these feelings of abandonment and uncertainty away. Help us become more aware of your presence and calm the storm that makes us feel insecure. You are our refuge, and we will wait on you. In the mighty name of Jesus, we pray. Amen.

Scriptures about Our Refuge

Psalm 121:4-8 (NIV) "Indeed he who watches over Israel will neither slumber nor sleep. The Lord watches over you, the Lord is your shade at your right hand; the sun will not harm you by day, nor the moon by night. The Lord will keep you from all harm, he will watch over your life; the Lord will watch over your coming and going both now, and forevermore."

Romans 8:28 (NIV) "And we know that in all things God works for the good of those who love him, who have been called according to his purpose."

Psalm 46:1 (NIV) "God is our refuge and strength, a very present help in trouble."

Submit

Write down a few things that cause uncertainty. Submit them to God.

_____

_____

_____

_____

Serve

Donate gently used clothes or luggage bags to a shelter.

SEEKING GOD ABOUT FINANCES

In my next book, I get pretty transparent about my finances and how I used to overspend on so many things. I was careless and wanted to keep us with the latest trends. As independent women, sometimes we are too dependent on keeping up with others or consumed with having whatever we want when we want. We should definitely enjoy what we earn however, we should do so in moderation. One of the biggest things that changed my life financially was tithing and giving faithfully. Tithing to the church as the word of God says and giving to others have blessed me tremendously. Whether you're hoping for a financial miracle, desiring to be a better steward, or just praying to stay on track, tithing faithfully can help you get there. Know that when you give God your first fruit by tithing, he will take care of you and give you the wisdom to handle what you have. Being stingy will produce more greed, but when you sow into others, you'll have immense joy.

Prayer Prompt

Holy Spirit, I ask that you cover our finances and help us to release them back to you. Help us to be consistent givers, investors, and women of wealth. Please help us research the right tools and programs that are the right fit for us to save and spend. We thank you for financial blessings and favor. We thank you for opening doors of increase and wealth. We praise you for doing exceedingly, abundantly, above all, we can ask, think, or imagine, as your word says in Ephesians 3:20. Father, we praise you that we will be blessed to be a blessing, and not just be lenders, but givers. Givers that don't look for anything in return because we know you have us! We pray these things in your name Jesus. Amen.

Scripture on Finances

Deuteronomy 9:12 (NIV) "But remember the Lord your God, for it is he who gives you the ability to produce wealth, and so confirms his covenant, which he swore to your ancestors, as it is today."

Luke 6:38 (NIV) "Give and it will be given to you. A good measure, pressed down, shaken together and running over, will be poured into your lap."

2 Corinthians 9:7 (NIV) "Each of you should give what you have decided in your heart to give, not reluctantly or under compulsion, for God loves a cheerful giver."

Submit

Write down three healthy financial habits you desire to have.

_____

_____

_____

_____

Serve

Pay for the person behind you when grabbing a meal or ask God to use you in meeting a financial need for someone.

SEEKING GOD FOR STABLE FRIENDSHIPS

Have you ever found yourself praying for friendships? It seems like the older we become, the harder some friendships become. We've probably all experienced friendships ending because of changes in maturity, salvation, or because of a disagreement. It's normal, some friendships end and it hurts when we disconnect from people that we've done life with. Friendships are important at every age, and it is good that we have someone to talk to, that knows us well and that holds us accountable. I believe stable friendships are attainable and if we notice a pattern of brokenness in this area, God can bring healing. Be open to the Holy Spirit revealing character flaws you may have. Be willing to think about the type of people you're allowing in your life, and why. Remember that the quality of your friendships are more important than the quantity, so be sure to cherish the friends you do have.

Prayer Prompt

Father, help us see the value in our friendships and not to glorify the ones we see on social media with groups of women. Help us rather to be satisfied with a few good friends that are genuine and that we cover and hold accountable. Help us to become better friends and listeners and develop our character even when we have a disagreement with our friends. We thank you for Godly friendships and that the enemy will not intervene. We thank you for lasting friendships and friendships that we will be gracious with. In Jesus' name. Amen.

Scriptures for Stable friendship

Proverbs 12:26 (NIV) "The righteous choose their friends carefully, but the way of the wicked leads them astray."

Psalm 133:1 (NIV) "How good and pleasant it is when God's people live together in unity."

1 Thessalonians 5:11(ESV) "Therefore encourage one another and build one another up, just as you are doing."

Romans 12:10 (NIV) "Be devoted to one another in love, honor one another above yourselves."

Submit

Write down a lesson or two that you've learned from past friendships and how it's helped you grow for new friendships.

_____

_____

_____

_____

Serve

Have a conversation with a friend, to see how you can become a better friend.

SEEKING GOD TO BE A SERVANT LEADER

There are many perks to being a leader, like receiving respect, looked up to, being respectfully feared, and seen as powerful. However, a servant leader is someone special that places the needs of others, as a priority, and serves them well. A servant leader is what Jesus wants us to be, not so that we can boast or brag, saying look what I've done, but to live as he lived. He desires to see the growth and reward that comes with being humble and thinking of the community, families, church members, and anyone we serve. When I think about a great female servant, a young lady from the Bible by the name of Esther comes to mind. She was appointed as queen but did not walk around high and mighty. Though she was met with challenges, she listened to her elder Mordecai and requested that her husband, the king, make changes on behalf of her people. Esther held the title of a leader but took the position of a servant. She risked speaking up for her people and allowed God to use her. I want to encourage you to serve from a place of humility, regardless of your status or accolades. God sees our hearts and the why behind all we do. I want to encourage you to speak up for others just as Esther did, and make a righteous impact. Read the book of Esther in the Bible and familiarize yourself with her story.

Prayer prompt

Father, we thank you for the opportunity to be a servant leader. We don't take this position for granted or to receive praise. Help us to take the focus off ourselves, to be givers and humble when it comes to serving. Help us serve well in our families, communities, and within our church. We thank you for the strength and grace it takes to serve and that we won't grow weary. Allow us to use the gifts you've placed in us as a way to serve and fulfill purpose. Thank you for helping us to discern the needs of others before they ask. We pray that we pour into the hearts and lives of your sons and daughters, as you pour into us. In Jesus' name. Amen.

Scriptures on Serving

Matthew 20:26-28 (NIV) "Instead, whoever wants to become great among you must be a servant, and whoever wants to be first must be your slave just as the Son of Man did not come to be served but to serve, and to give his life as a ransom for many."

Galatians 5:13 (NIV) "You my brothers and sisters, were called to be free. But do not use your freedom to indulge in flesh; rather serve one another humbly in love."

1 Peter 4:10 (NIV) "Each of you should use whatever gift you have received to serve others, as faithful stewards of God's grace in its various forms."

1 Peter 4:11 (NIV) "If anyone speaks, they should do so as one who speaks the very words of God. If anyone serves, they should do so with the strength God provides, so that in all things God may be praised through Jesus Christ. To him be the glory and the power for ever and ever. Amen."

Submit

Give over any pride or plans that you've had in mind. Write down how you plan to become a better servant leader.

_____

_____

_____

_____

Serve

Look into ways you can serve in a different country virtually or in person.

SEEKING TO PLEASE GOD

In the last entry, I wrote about Esther and felt the need to mention her once again. You see, although God is not actually mentioned in the book of Esther, after reading, you can see that his glory and grace is in her life. Each time she had a request for her husband, the king, she went before him, saying "If it pleases the king," then she made her request known. I believe we can really learn something from this and apply it to our own lives. While Jesus is our daddy, best friend, and one that we can talk openly to, he is also a sovereign king. When we have a request, we shouldn't bring arrogance as if God has to do anything. Instead, we should come with a submissive heart. We must desire to please him, and the outcome of what we desire must please him as well. When we live a life of pleasing Jesus, so many things will fall into place in our lives. When we have selfish ambitions looking to please ourselves, we're met with self-destruction. I want to challenge you today to start each day asking God, "How can I serve you today?" "How can I make you proud?"

Prayer Prompt

Lord, it is our desire to please you. We know every day won't be perfect, but we will seek you for strength and mercy. Help us to start our day seeking you first, finding ways of serving you throughout the day with how we interact with others, and how we work. I thank you for changing our hearts and our desires to become your desires for us. In Jesus' name. Amen.

Scriptures on Pleasing God

Psalms 37:5 (NIV) "Commit your way unto the Lord; trust in him and he will do this: He will make your righteous reward shine like the dawn, your vindication like the noonday sun."

Hebrews 11:6 (NIV) "And without faith it is impossible to please Him, for he who comes to God must believe that He is and that a rewarder of those who seek Him."

Romans 12:1(KJV) "Therefore I urge you. Brethren, by the mercies of God, to present your bodies a living and holy sacrifice, acceptable to God, which is your spiritual service of worship."

Romans 8:7-8 (NIV) "The mind governed by the flesh is hostile to God; it does not submit to
God's law, nor can it do so. Those who are in the realm of the flesh cannot please God."

Submit

Write down two ways you plan to please God.

_____

_____

_____

_____

Serve

Show someone a small or large act of kindness just because.

SEEKING GOD WHEN YOU FEEL UNWORTHY

There's a woman in the Bible who knew herself to be a sinner, and the townsmen knew it as well. When this woman meets Jesus, she "stood before him at his feet weeping, she began to wet his feet with her tears." Luke 7:37 NIV. I believe this woman was so overwhelmed with his presence and couldn't help but think about her past and lifestyle. The Bible goes on to say that Jesus forgave her sins and that "her faith saved her." This woman gave God what she had; she brought a surrendered heart, kissed his feet, and poured perfume on them. Feeling unworthy may keep us from ministry, being a light to those around us, and can ultimately have us self-consumed. This is why it's important that we find a space to worship Jesus and cry out to him. He saw us as worthy to die on the cross for all our sins and will not hold back his grace for us. There isn't a sin too big that he would say, "No, that one I didn't die for." You are worthy, and as you cry tears and pour out your love on him like perfume, he will forgive you and help you live a fulfilled life of freedom.

Prayer Prompt

Father, we thank you that in you, we are blameless! There is nothing too dirty, nothing too destructive, nothing too harmful that we've done that you won't forgive when we are sincere. You wipe the tears from our eyes, and you restore us when we feel ashamed. Father, we cast down the negative thoughts that keep us trapped in contentment. Thank you for your saving grace that makes us worthy. In Jesus' name. Amen.

Scriptures about your worth

Jeremiah 1:5 (NIV) "Before I formed you in the womb, I knew you before you were born, I set you apart."

Jeremiah 29:11(NIV) "For I know the plans I have for you, plans to prosper you and not to harm you, plans to give you hope and a future."

Luke 7:38 (NIV) "As she stood behind him at his feet weeping, she began to wet his feet with her tears. Then she wiped them with her hair, kissed them and poured perfume on them."

Submit

Lay the feeling of unworthiness at his feet. Write down what makes you feel this way and listen for the Lord's response.

_____

_____

_____

_____

Serve

Remind someone else of their worthiness to God. Share in a small group how you are discovering your worth in him.

SEEKING GOD WHEN YOU FEEL UNSEEN

I know all too well what it's like to be in a crowded room but feel overlooked and unseen. I've been the rejected woman by someone I thought truly cared about me. I've felt like an outsider around family and friends. There are times I've wondered if God really sees me. Yes, I know he made me, yet at times, I have honestly felt as if he's forgotten about me. I'm so glad now I know for sure that he sees me and loves me daily! There's a woman in the Bible that you may or may not have overlooked yourself. She's the mother Ishmael, or as the Bible says, "the handmaid of Abraham and Sara." Her name is Hagar, and she was brought into what some would say is a messy situation. After Hagar conceived Ishmael, she fled Sara because she was being mistreated. I can only imagine all the thoughts that must have ran through her mind being pregnant and feeling used and overlooked. The bible tells us, God sent an angel to her and shared with her the promises over her and her son's life. She knew then that she was seen and known. El Roi meaning the God who sees me, met with her at her lowest point, and directed her on what to do next. Daughters of God, it's time to dismiss those feelings of being overlooked. This same God sees and knows you well. If he has you hidden, then know there's purpose attached to it. Trust that you are fully known, and completely loved.

Prayer Prompt

Lord, thank you for covering us and seeing us daily. We can rest in knowing that we matter to you and that you've placed people in our lives that truly see us and accept us. Help us, trust that every rejection is just redirection and a part of your plan. Release us from the desire to be seen or important to those who do not serve purpose in our lives. We trust that you will open the right doors and close the wrong ones. No longer will we try to manipulate or maneuver situations or people to be seen. Thank you, Lord, for keeping us hidden when we feel we should be in the spotlight. In Jesus' name. Amen.

Scriptures to Know God Sees You

Psalms 139:1-3 (NIV) "You have searched me, Lord, and you know me. You know when I sit and when I rise; you perceive my thoughts from afar. You discern my going out and my lying down; you are familiar with all my ways."

Isaiah 40:11(NIV) "He tends to his flock like a shepherd; He gathers the lambs in his arms and carries them close to his heart; he gently leads those that have young."

Psalm 121:3 (NIV) "He will not let your foot slip, he who watches over you will not slumber."

Luke 12:7 (NIV) "Indeed, the very hairs of your head are all numbered. Don't be afraid; you are worth more than many sparrows."

Submit

Write about your current state of confidence. Submit those feelings to God.

_____

_____

_____

_____

Serve

Reach out to an elderly relative, family friend, or church member. Remind them that they are seen and loved.

SEEKING GOD FOR HIDDEN ISSUES

In Luke 8:43, the Bible introduces us to a woman with an issue of blood. She's described as a woman who's been bleeding for twelve years. She most likely gave up hope, after being told there was no cure. Yet she heard about the healer who was visiting her town and made her way to him. This woman, even with all her possible pain, soaked clothes, and insecurities made her way into a crowd to find Jesus for her healing. Verse 44 says "she came up behind him and touched the edge of his cloak, and immediately her bleeding stopped (NIV). Daughter, you may not be facing this particular issue, but what issue comes to your mind when you think of reaching out to Jesus? Some of us have been battling negative thinking, anxiety, strongholds, depression, and chronic pain for many years. Your family may not have been willing to go out of their way to be healed from the generational curse, but you can. You may not see other women laying prostrate at the altar, but don't let that stop you. Your significant other or children may not be used to seeing you speak in tongues or pressing into his presence, but you can start. Bring all your issues to him; let your faith make you well.

Prayer Prompt

Lord, today we reach out to touch the hem of your garment through prayer. We cannot thrive with these internal battles. We know you can make us whole. We come with faith, and expectation, for the healing of our minds, hearts, and bodies. We ask that you heal the unspoken issues within us and our families. Thank you Lord, for canceling the assignment of the enemy that keeps us in doubt. We will be made whole, in Jesus' name. Amen.

Scriptures for Hidden Issues

Jeremiah 17:14 (NIV) "Heal me, Lord and I will be healed; save me and I will be saved, for you are the one I praise."

Colossians 2:9 (NIV) "For in Christ all the fullness of the Deity lives in bodily form, and in Christ you have been brought to fullness."

Luke 8:47-48 (KJV) "And when the woman saw that she was not hidden, she came trembling, and falling down before him, she declared unto him before all the people for what cause she had touched him, and how she was healed immediately. And he said unto her, Daughter, be of good comfort: thy faith hath made thee whole; go in peace."

Submit

Write down three truths you've been hiding in your heart yet not saying directly to the Lord. Allow God to speak to your heart about how he's healing them.

_____

_____

_____

_____

Serve

Join a Bible study group and help other women come out of hiding.

SEEKING GOD FOR CREATIVITY

Ladies, we are creative! God created us to bear children, care for children, paint, act, cook, sing, praise dance, and the list goes on. We may not find ourselves in every category, but the beauty of being God's handiwork is that he created us to be creative. He gave us wild imagination to carry out what he placed inside of us. Whether your desire is to move up within a company you work for or become a full-time entrepreneur, God wants to help you level up in your skill and creativity. He wants to see us develop and grow our skills. He wants to see us thrive and move up in the company, open our own businesses and studios, create multiple streams of income, and more. For some of us, being a stay-at-home mom or a caregiver in this season is still an area in which God can bring income, peace, and creativity. There are no limits on our creative Father; he can provide the motivation you need, he can and will awaken the dreams you thought were lost or you've outgrown.

Prayer Prompt

Father, we thank you that you will enlarge our territory with creativity. Let it just flow from us and within our imagination. You created us in your image and likeness, giving us great hope that we, too, can be creative. We praise you for more ideas, ways to expand knowledge, and more opportunities for us to grow. Father, help those of us who have given up on our talents and gifts. Awaken creativity inside of us that we put aside. Help us to become motivated and push past any obstacles we may face. In the mighty name of Jesus. Amen.

Scriptures for Creatives

1 Timothy 4:14 (NIV) "Do not neglect your gift, which was given you through prophecy when the body of elders laid their hands on you."

Exodus 31:3 (NIV) "And I have filled him with the Spirit of God, with wisdom and understanding, with knowledge and with all kinds of skills."

1 Corinthians 7:7 (ESV) "I wish that all were as I myself am. But each has his own gift from God, one of one kind and one of another."

Romans 12:6-8 (NIV) "We have different gifts, according to the grace given to each of us. If your gift is prophesying, then prophesy in accordance with your faith; if it is serving, then serve; if it is teaching, then teach; if it is to encourage, then give encouragement; if it is to lead, do it diligently; if it is to show mercy, do it cheerfully."

Submit

Write down what your gifts are and ask God to show you how to use them for the kingdom.

_____

_____

_____

_____

Serve

Share your creativity within a small group at work, church, or for your community.

SEEKING GOD FOR WISDOM

There is nothing quite like wisdom. The book of Proverbs is full of scriptures on it, and I love that the Bible personifies wisdom as a female, but I guess that's a little biased. Regardless, as we make daily decisions, from small to life-changing, we are in need of applying wisdom. It's vital that we seek God through prayer and wise council such as elders, parents, and friends. Seeking wisdom is a practice of humility and acceptance that we don't have all the answers.

Prayer Prompt

Father, help your daughters with making the right decisions that concern them. Help us to think about who our decisions will affect and how they will be affected. Allow us to think about the beginning, middle, and ending and not just instant gratification. We thank you that we can come to you when we are troubled or unsure, and you will guide us on whether to move or be still. Let us be open to receiving the advice of wise council, whether young or old and not to allow pride to turn wisdom away. In Jesus' name. Amen.

Scriptures on Wisdom

Ephesians 1:17 (NIV) "I keep asking that the God of our Lord Jesus Christ, the glorious Father, may give you the Spirit of wisdom and revelation so that you may know him better."

Psalm 111:10 (NIV) "The fear of the Lord is the beginning of wisdom, all who follow his precepts have good understanding."

James 3:17 (NIV) "But the wisdom that comes from heaven is first of all pure; then peace-loving, considerate, submissive, full of mercy, and good fruit, impartial and sincere."

Proverbs 1:5-6 (NIV) "Let the wise listen and add to their learning, and let the discerning get guidance for understanding proverbs and parables."

Submit

Write two approaches you'll use to grow in wisdom.

_____

_____

_____

_____

Serve

Intercede on behalf of the mentors in your life.

SEEKING GOD FOR FORGIVING OTHERS

When we know we've sinned, we look to God for forgiveness. We expect or at least desire that he will open his loving arms, embrace us, and no longer bring up the past. Do we share these characteristics with others? When someone hurts us or makes a bad choice, do we provide grace? Is it depending on what they've done, or do we instantly put on bitterness and block them from our lives? I believe God wants us to really take a look at these questions and answer them honestly. I know how easy it is for us as women to hold grudges, hold on to bitterness, block, and find a way to soothe our own pain and protect ourselves. But God has called us to forgive. Forgiveness doesn't make us forget, nor does it make us weak. God not only requests this of us, he actually commands that we give forgiveness to others, just as we desire it. He doesn't say forgive only if you feel it's right, only if it suits you, only if you think you can do it. No, he wants you to take the time to change your heart for those who've failed you. Oh, I know this is easier said than done, but it is possible through him and with him.

Prayer Prompt

Father God, please help us to let go of the bitterness that's actually hurting us and holding us back in certain areas of our lives. Teach us how to extend grace; and show us who to love from a distance. Help us to forgive those, who haven't apologized to us. This journey to forgive is not easy for us and it's easier to stay offended, yet we are tired of carrying this burden, replaying hurtful scenarios, and holding grudges. We thank you for forgiving us and for healing our hearts so that we will do the same for others. In Jesus' name. Amen.

Scriptures on Forgiveness

Matthew 6:15 (NIV) "But if you do not forgive others their sins, your Father will not forgive your sins."

Proverbs 24:17 (NIV) "Do not gloat when your enemy falls; when they stumble, do not let your heart rejoice."

Colossians 3:13 (ESV) "Bearing with one another and, if one has a complaint against another, forgiving each other; as the Lord has forgiven you, so you also must forgive."

Submit

Write down your truth about forgiving others. Where are you on the journey to forgiveness?

_____

_____

_____

_____

Serve

Offer forgiveness to someone you were once bitter with.

SEEKING GOD WITH GRATITUDE

When is the last time that you've thanked God for all he's done for you? Not because it's your birthday or a special occasion. He deserves the honor and glory at all times; not just when everything is going your way. I want to encourage you to spend time in worship, thanking God with a grateful heart. Give him praises, tell him thank you when you get in and out of your car, or when you swipe your debit card. Begin to look at the ordinary things, as extraordinary and walk in gratitude. Be grateful when there's a pile of dishes and loads of laundry. Thank him when there's a flat tire. Yes, even a flat tire because you never know what he may be protecting you from. It's time to become more aware of his presence then your problems. Give thanks.

Prayer Prompt

Father God, we thank you for another day, for life, health, and strength. Lord, if we are feeling weak, we thank you for strength, we praise you for making a way when it seems like there's no way. We are grateful for the doors you've closed and the relationships you caused to end. We give you praise just because of who you are and for loving us. We thank you for what you've done, and what you will do. In Jesus' name. Amen.

Scriptures on Gratitude

Psalm 150:6 (NIV) "Let everything that has breath praise the Lord."

Hebrews 13:15 (NIV) "Through Jesus, therefore, let us continually offer to God a sacrifice of praise for the fruit of lips that openly profess his name."

Psalms 9:1(KJV) "I will praise thee, O Lord, with my whole heart; I will shew forth thy marvelous works.

Submit

Create a gratitude list of at least seven things, and give God praise for them.

_____

_____

_____

_____

Serve

Send a thank you card or provide an act of gratitude to someone you're grateful for.

SEEKING GOD TO BREAK GENERATIONAL CURSES

Sometimes what we grew up seeing, we repeat. Our worldview and way of thinking may be a result of cycles from our father and mothers' side of the family or both. When we entered this world, we entered a sinful world and became sinful people. It's only through salvation that we are saved, yet even after we've given our hearts to God, there is work to be done. We literally must allow him to come in like a surgeon to change us. Our Father is the perfect gentleman, not an intruder, so we must allow him to do the work. When we back away from him, then we are saying we aren't ready. In those moments he will wait patiently, for us to let him into the areas of our lives that caused the cycles. Some cycles took years to form, and became second nature, so understand that there will also be a journey to your healing. Once he begins to break those cycles, you may feel uncomfortable, and out of place. You may lose friends or have family look at you differently. I encourage you to keep moving forward, don't look back. God will deliver and set you free.

Prayer Prompt

Lord, help us become aware of the things that feel normal but are generational curses. Help us break out of the old mindsets and old way of doing things. Let us become the first of our family to break cycles; let us set the example for those who come after us. Help us to live a life of legacy and to step out of our fears and comfort zone. Let us stop caring about the looks we may receive from family members, or the harsh words of those who may become intimidated by our change. Help us to be women who aren't scared of allowing you to break things off us for the sake of ourselves and families. Whether in our teens, twenties, thirties, forties, fifties, sixties, or older we thank you for setting us free. In your precious name, we pray. Amen.

Scriptures to Break Generational Curses

John 10:10 (KJV) "The thief cometh not, but for to steal, and to kill and destroy: I am to come that they might have life, and that they might have it more abundantly."

James 5:16 (NIV) "Therefore confess your sins to each other and pray for each other so that you may be healed. The prayer of a righteous person is powerful and effective."

Romans 8:2 (KJV) "For the law of the Spirit of life in Christ Jesus hath made me free from the law of sin and death.

Submit

Write about a cycle that you desire to see broken.

_____

_____

_____

_____

Serve

As God helps you break cycles, share the process to help free a non-believer.

SEEKING GOD FOR LOVE

When I was younger, I asked God into my heart. I repeated what I was told, sung all the kiddy songs, and acted in the Christmas and Easter plays. Once I was a little older, I was baptized a time or two, and repented every Sunday. I was saved by grace, but something was missing. I was taught about God's love throughout my life, but didn't really receive his love until I learned, I needed a relationship with him. Now, of course, he's loved me all along however, I wasn't open or aware of it like I am now. It would take more than my mom's testimony and more than what the pastor said. After receiving salvation, you'll need to gain a real relationship with him. Have you ever stopped and thought God really loves me? You are daughter to him, the apple of his eye, and he's not looking down on you to judge, or punish. I know that there are religious sermons that have made you feel like you'll never be enough. You've felt like an outcast because of your style choices, people have judged you when they should've reached out to mentor you and you worry if there's enough you can do. The love of Jesus is available to you, even if you feel like the black sheep of the family, he will search for you. Like a groom waiting for his bride, he wants to be your first love. I pray that this book encourages you to come to him, just as you are. Spiritual growth takes time, discipline, and patience. Don't stop seeking, reading scripture, submitting, or serving. His love is for you.

Prayer prompt

Father God, please allow your daughters to feel the warmth of your love. Allow us to know your kind and caring nature. Heal the places where hurt resides, help us to trust again, and breathe without the anxieties of being rejected. May we find a secret place to meet and fall in love with you. Help us not to go astray or search for love in the wrong places when we are weary. Lift our countenance and overwhelm us with true love from you. In Jesus' name. Amen.

Scriptures on God's Love

Ephesians 5:1-2 (NIV) "Follow God's example, therefore, as dearly loved children and walk in the way of love, just as Christ loved us and gave himself up for us as a fragrant offering and sacrifice to God."

1 John 4:18 (KJV) "There is no fear in love; but perfect love drives out fear, because fear has to do with punishment. The one who fears is not made perfect in love."

1 Corinthians 13:4-7 (NIV) "Love is patient, love is kind. It does not envy, it does not boast, it is not proud. It does not dishonor others, it is not self-seeking, it is not easily angered, it keeps no record of wrongs. Love does not delight in evil but rejoices with the truth. It always protects, always trust, always hopes, always perseveres."

Submit

Write down three of your favorite attributes of love and how the Father has shown them to you.

_____

_____

_____

_____

Serve

Take one or more attributes of love and show them to others, even when your feelings tell you differently.

Keeping Up with the Author

Visit Kelley's website to discover her Music, Ministry and Blogs at kelleyhallmusic.com

Stay up to date with The Grown Woman's Guide by following Kelley's Instagram @kelleyhallmusic and subscribe to her YouTube channel: kelleyhallmusic.

www.ingramcontent.com/pod-product-compliance
Lightning Source LLC
Chambersburg PA
CBHW060122050426
42448CB00010B/1994